Christian Coffee Table Book of Grace

Beautiful Images and Reflections Inspired by the Book of Psalms, the Gospels, and the Beauty of Faith

———⚬❦⚬———

ETERNAL WORD EDITION

Table of Contents

Introduction

Welcome. This book was created as a quiet space for reflection, a companion for morning coffee, an evening pause, or any moment when your heart longs for stillness. Within these pages you will find meditative words paired with simple, striking images, because beauty often hides in the smallest details. Together they invite you to breathe, to look, and to listen for the presence of God in your everyday life.

Why These Words Matter

In a noisy world, a moment of spiritual pause offers a steady voice. These reflections are meant to remind you of who you are, why you were created, and how deeply you are loved. Even a brief reading can reorient a restless mind, renew hope, and spark gratitude. They are not simply thoughts to ponder; they are invitations to transformation: gentle prompts to let God's Spirit guide your heart and bring peace to your day.

Images of God's Presence

The visuals throughout this book are black and white by design. Stripped of color, each image highlights God's light, shadow, and form, encouraging you to notice the quiet details we often miss. You will see nature, moments of family connection, places of worship, and simple signs of love, because God's presence is not confined to any one place or time. He is in the rustle of trees, the warmth of an embrace, the lines of sacred architecture, and the everyday gestures of care.

An Invitation to Reflect

This is not a book to read once and set aside. Open it anywhere. Let a single thought rest in your mind or allow a longer passage to guide a prayer or spark a conversation. Each pairing of image and text is meant to slow you down and draw your spirit toward God, toward life, hope, and the quiet mystery of His grace. Return to these pages whenever you need stillness and let them remind you that even the smallest moment of reflection can open the heart to something eternal.

May these words and images remind you that the Lord is near, that His beauty surrounds you, and that His love endures forever.

Light & Hope

When the first light spills across the horizon, it carries a quiet promise: God's love renews every morning. No darkness of yesterday can withstand the brilliance of His mercy or dim the glow of His compassion. The rising sun reminds us that His forgiveness is not earned but freely given: a fresh beginning offered to every heart willing to receive it. As the sky warms with colour, so our souls are invited to awaken, to release the weight of regret and breathe in the hope of a new day. Each dawn is a gentle sermon of grace, whispering that God's faithfulness outlasts every night and that His love will meet us again, brighter and deeper than before.

_____

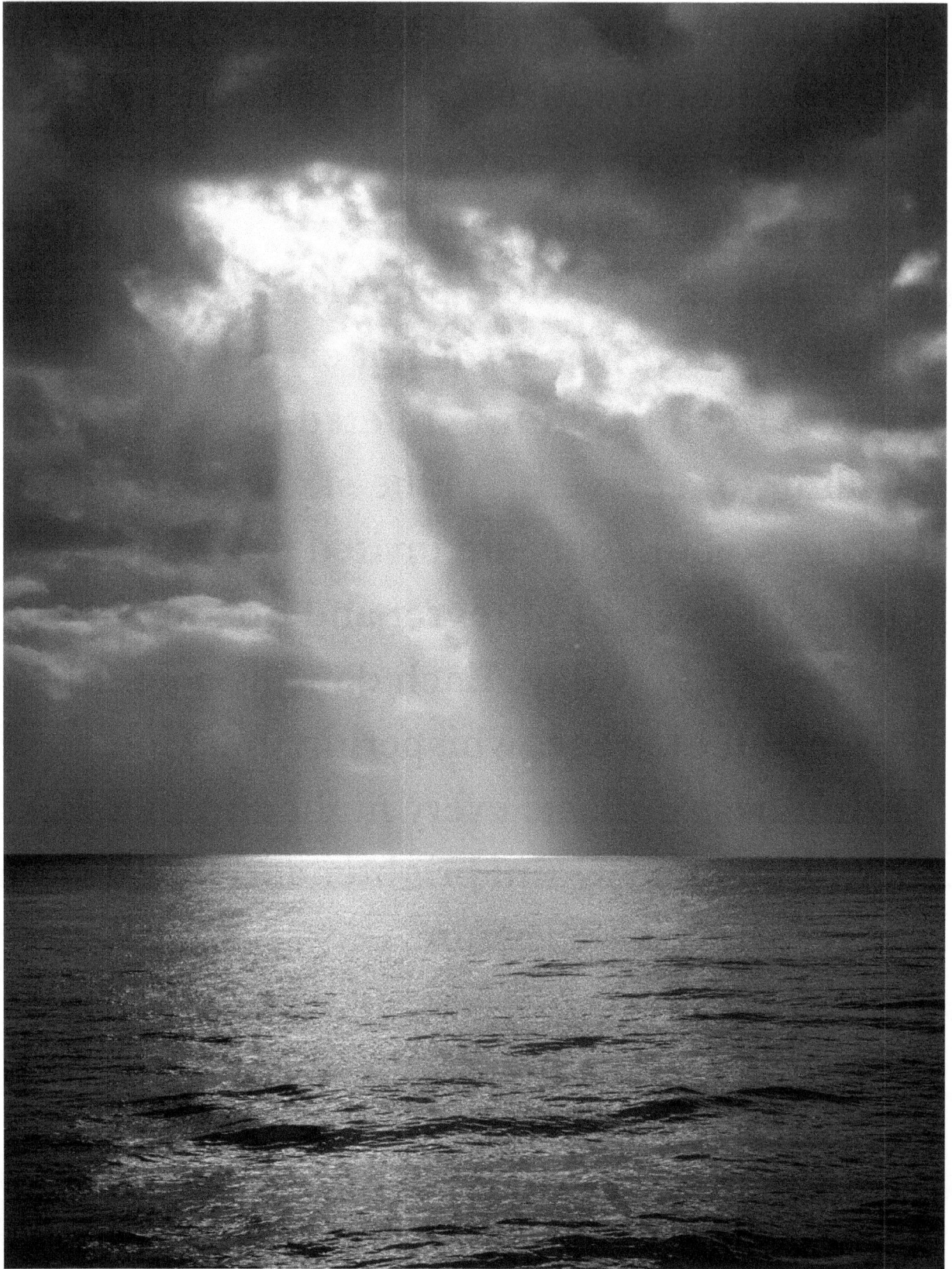

Life's road can twist through valleys of doubt and confusion, yet the Lord's light never wavers. Even when the path is hidden, His radiance reaches beyond what we can see, leading us safely home.

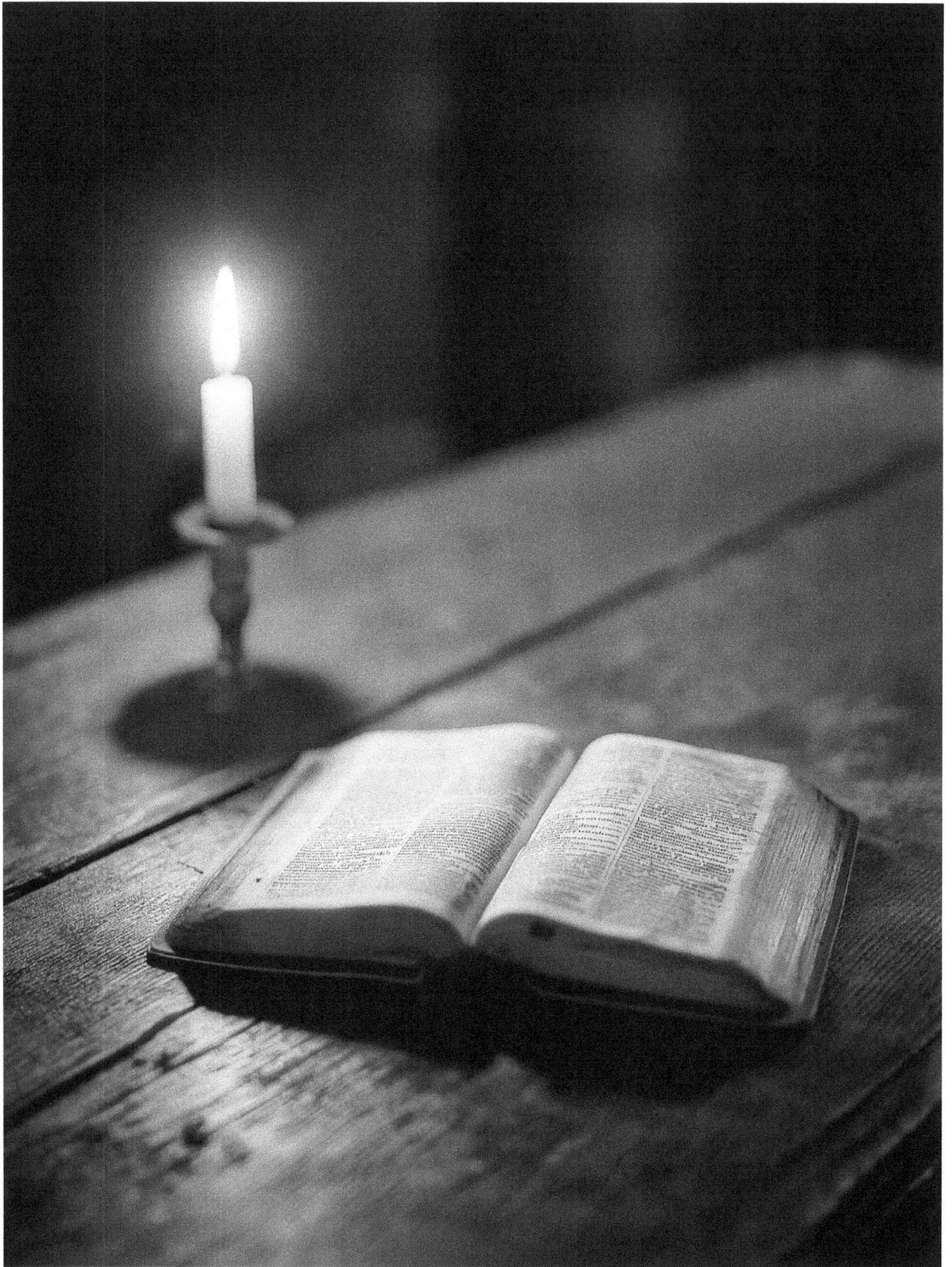

Clouds may veil the heavens, yet the morning still arrives with quiet certainty and a light that cannot be held back. So, it is with the Lord's faithfulness, often unseen but never absent, steadily breaking through every layer of doubt with the gentle brilliance of His promises. His presence does not depend on clear skies or easy days; it moves like the sure rhythm of dawn, reaching us even when our hearts feel shadowed. Each new sunrise is His reminder that grace is stronger than fear and that His love will not fail, carrying us into the day with renewed hope and unshakable peace.

When dawn brushes the sky, remember: God renews mercy with every sunrise. Yesterday's worries fade in the warmth of His steadfast love.

14

Light is the first language of creation, the quiet unveiling of God's presence that reaches into every corner of our lives. Even when the sky is heavy with clouds or the heart feels dim, His brightness moves silently through the shadows, revealing paths we could not see. Hope awakens in that radiance, not as a sudden blaze but as a steady glow that strengthens with each breath of trust. It reminds us that no season of doubt lasts forever, and no wound is beyond the touch of divine healing. Each morning, the world is reborn in a spectrum of colour and warmth, a gentle assurance that new beginnings are always possible. Let this light draw you forward with courage, for the One who spoke it into existence continues to shine within you, carrying a promise that outlives every night and turns even the darkest valley into a place of quiet, steadfast hope.

Christ walks before us as a lamp to each uncertain step. Even when the path twists through shadow, His radiance leads us home.

Hope seldom shouts; it waits, steady and unseen. Beneath winter soil God is already stirring life toward spring, weaving renewal where eyes see only stillness. Though you may notice only bare branches now, trust the Creator who brings beauty in its season and life out of what seemed lifeless. His timing is never hurried, yet it never fails. Even in the coldest days, His quiet work is shaping tomorrow's blossoms and preparing your heart to rejoice when the first green shoots break through the earth.

———————————————————

No darkness can silence the quiet strength of hope. The empty tomb declares that every long night must yield to morning.

A day is coming when night will vanish, and God's glory will be our endless sun, shining brighter than every star and softer than the gentlest dawn. On that radiant morning all sorrow will dissolve, every wound will be healed, and every tear will be lovingly dried by the hand of the One who calls us His own. Time itself will bow to eternity, and the faithful will stand in the warmth of a love that never wanes. The songs of heaven will rise like a river of light, and joy will pulse through creation with unbroken harmony. Let that promise steady your heart and give you courage for today, a quiet joy that no darkness can steal and no shadow can dim: a sure hope that even now begins to glow within the soul.

Wisdom & Guidance

Seek the Lord in every decision and He will steady your steps. His wisdom lights the road even when you cannot see the next turn.

The Spirit of God is a faithful instructor, quietly weaving lessons through the ordinary rhythms of life. He speaks in moments we might overlook: a sudden insight during routine work, a nudge of conscience when choices weigh heavy, the gentle clarity that comes in stillness. Even trials become sacred classrooms when we welcome His counsel, for every challenge carries wisdom waiting to be discovered. He does not lecture with harshness but corrects with a love that heals and a patience that never tires. Over days and years. He shapes the heart, refining motives, strengthening faith, and drawing out a character fit for eternity. In His guidance we find not only direction but transformation, as He molds our lives into a living reflection of the One who sent Him.

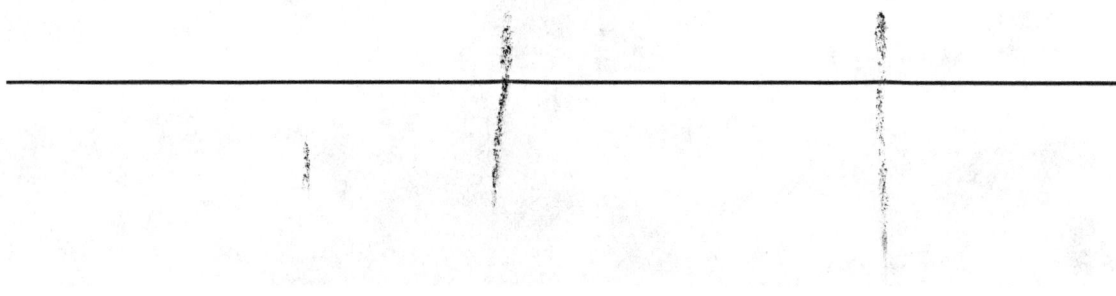

God often speaks in gentle whispers. Pause and listen: His guidance meets the heart that waits in stillness.

Especially when the night comes and it's hard to see, let the Lord be your compass and light — eventually, by the end of the night, He will lead you exactly where you're supposed to be. Breath.

When confusion clouds your path and every option blurs, Christ remains the unwavering way. In the stillness of prayer, kneel and invite His wisdom, knowing that His voice often comes like a quiet dawn rather than a sudden flash. Trust that the answer—though it may unfold slowly—will arrive with perfect timing and a purpose greater than you can yet imagine. His leading is gentle but sure, a light that reaches past uncertainty and fear. As you follow, anxiety begins to loosen its grip, and the peace of His presence settles deeper than any storm, assuring you that you are never alone and never lost in His care.

Scripture is a lamp for the mind and a shield for the soul. Open its pages and let truth illuminate your day.

Our Savior knows His sheep, and His sheep know His voice. Amid the noise of a restless world, His call remains steady and kind, never hurried or harsh. He walks before us with patient love, guiding each step and watching every turn. When we pause to listen and trust His leading, we discover green pastures for the soul, still waters that calm our fears, and a joy no wandering can steal: a peace that endures far beyond the valleys and hills of this life.

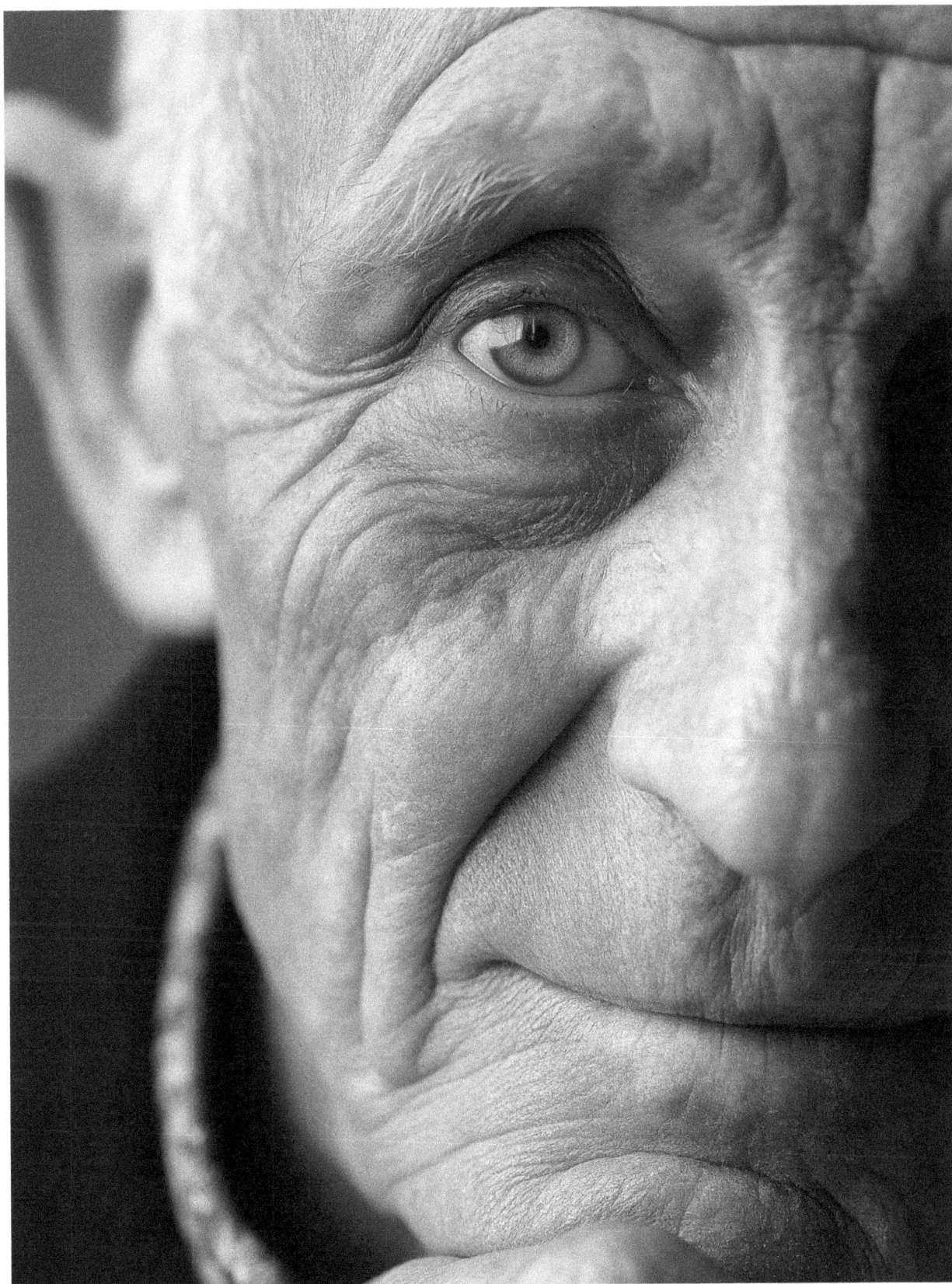

An old man's weathered years remind us that wisdom is the patient guidance of God, shaping a life through seasons of waiting and trust.

Every verse of Scripture carries a map of grace, charting the path of God's love through the hills and valleys of life. As you read and linger over its words, the Holy Spirit draws lines of courage and wisdom across your soul, shaping your thoughts and steadying your heart. In moments of choice or uncertainty, these living words rise within you, offering strength for decisions both great and small. The Word does not merely inform; it transforms, softening what is hard, healing what is broken, and guiding every willing heart toward the bright horizon of God's perfect will.

Rows of quiet shelves remind us that God's Word is the true treasure: wisdom that lights the mind and guides the heart.

Among rolling hills the shepherd walks, every step a quiet promise of protection and care. His voice carries across the pasture, steady and familiar, and the sheep follow because they know the sound of love that never fails. In the same way, Christ calls to each of us, guiding through confusion, guarding against danger, and leading toward rest. When the path grows steep or the night deepens, His presence remains sure, a staff of comfort and a light that never fades. Under His watch we lack nothing, for His guidance is perfect and His mercy without end.

An open book rests like a doorway of light, inviting you to meet the living Word where God speaks new wisdom into every willing heart.

Service & Compassion

To serve is not only to give things but to give ourselves. Sitting with the lonely, listening without hurry, and praying without ceasing are quiet offerings that reflect the ministry of Christ, who came close to the broken and called them beloved. Presence is a holy act that tells the weary they are not forgotten and reminds us of that God Himself dwells with those who hurt. It means setting aside distractions, sharing silence without trying to fix, and offering a steady heart when words are few. In such moments we embody the love of Emmanuel, whose comfort stays gentle and sure, a living testimony that heaven leans close and every soul is cherished by the Lord.

True service begins where self-interest ends, as we offer our hands for Christ to use in quiet acts of love.

When we shoulder another's burden, we enter the fellowship of Christ Himself. He carries the world's sorrow, and in joining Him we discover a joy that suffering cannot quench and a strength beyond our own. Service may tire the body, but it renews the spirit, teaching us that every shared load lightens both hearts. In the mystery of His kingdom, what we carry for another becomes a gift we ourselves receive: deep friendship, unexpected courage, and the quiet assurance that we are walking in the very footsteps of our Lord.

Even the smallest kindness, given in Jesus' name, carries eternal weight and reflects the generosity of His heart.

True compassion is not loud or hurried. It listens, waits, and moves with the steady rhythm of God's own love. In patient service we find the miracle of transformation: both giver and receiver are changed, and the world catches a glimpse of the kingdom where kindness reigns and mercy have no end. Compassion bends low to lift another, reflecting the heart of Jesus who knelt to wash the feet of His friends. It is in these humble moments that eternity touches earth and God's love is felt most clearly.

Compassion is the heartbeat of the gospel: Mercy flowing freely because God first poured His Mercy into us.

Compassion is love refusing to stay still. It moves toward the hungry, the grieving, the overlooked. Each step toward another in need is a step into the very heart of God, where mercy becomes action and grace becomes bread for the soul. When we move in love, we carry the fragrance of Christ into places that have known only silence and despair. Our service becomes a living testimony that the Savior still walks among the hurting, inviting them to taste His goodness through our hands and our willingness to go where others will not.

A single act of quiet kindness can speak louder than a thousand words, revealing Christ's love where it is least expected.

Peace & Eternity

Eternity hums in the quiet air, a gentle note of love that never fades and never ends.

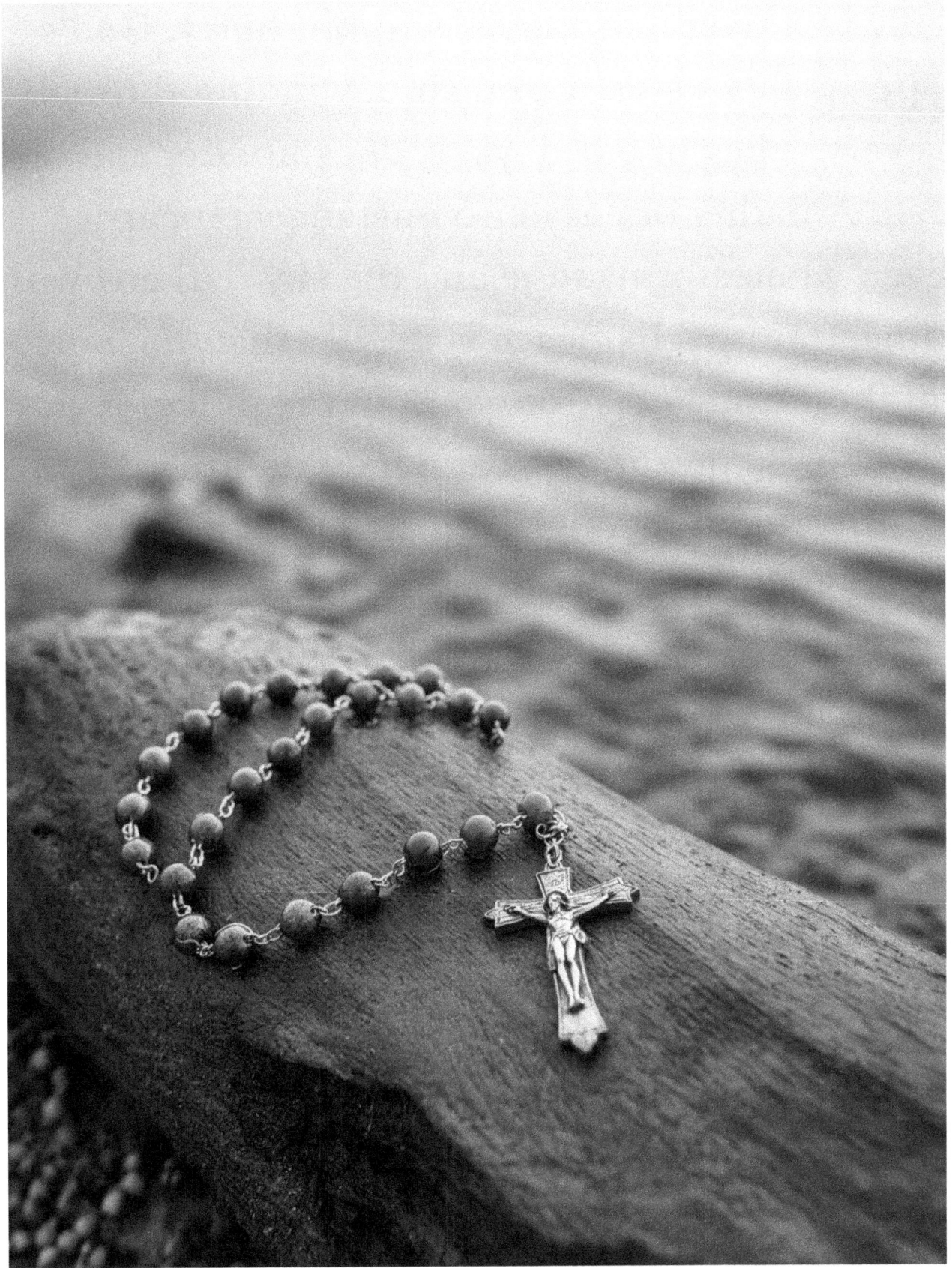

Like a river that moves without hurry, God's peace flows steady and sure, winding through every valley of our days. It does not depend on calm weather or easy circumstances; it carries us even when storms rage and the sky darkens with uncertainty. His peace is deeper than the noise of the world and stronger than the pull of fear, a quiet current that cannot be dammed or diverted. When we lean into His presence, anxiety loosens its grip, and our hearts learn to rest in the assurance that His eternal love surrounds every breath and every tomorrow. This river never runs dry. It refreshes weary spirits, smooths the rough stones of our worry, and leads us toward the vast ocean of His everlasting care, where our souls are finally and forever at home.

Christ offers a rest the world cannot give, a deep and lasting peace that remains when the noise fades and every striving comes to stillness, a calm that steadies the soul even in the midst of life's storms..

God has written eternity on the human heart, and every longing we feel for lasting love is a whisper of that truth. We sense it in the beauty that feels too deep for words, in friendships that we wish could never end, and in the quiet ache for something more than this passing world. Christ fulfills that yearning, offering life that death cannot diminish and a joy that will outlast the stars themselves. His resurrection is the pledge that time limits are not the final story. In Him, every moment of faith and every act of love is drawn into a future without end, a Forever that begins even now, in the steady hope of His presence.

Lift your eyes to the quiet night and count the stars if you can. Each glimmer is a reminder: the same God who scattered these lights across the sky keeps your life within His eternal dawn.

Beyond the noise of cities and the hum of restless hearts burns a quiet flame that never dims. It is the light of Christ, constant and unbound by time, warming the coldest night and outlasting the brightest star. Step close and feel its steady glow: it neither flickers nor fades. In that unending warmth the soul discovers a love deeper than grief and a calm stronger than fear, a radiant promise that the life we know is only the doorway to a forever filled with His presence.

When the first light spills across the earth, it carries the hush of eternity. In that golden silence, heaven leans close and the soul tastes the peace that has no ending.

Love & Grace

Across the hush of open fields, the presence of God moves like a soft breeze: steady, unseen, yet unmistakable. His love calls us onward with a patience that never rushes, shaping each moment with quiet purpose. It is not the path beneath our feet that matters most, but the nearness of the One who walks beside us. In His company, every step, whether through sunlight or shadow, becomes a lesson in grace, a reminder that His care is wider than the sky and deeper than our fears. Here the heart discovers that true direction is not found in maps or milestones, but in the faithful love that guides, restores, and brings us safely home.

God's love does not pause or weaken; it holds every soul with a tenderness that never lets go. Through joy and sorrow, His arms remain open, steady, and sure: an eternal embrace that nothing can break.

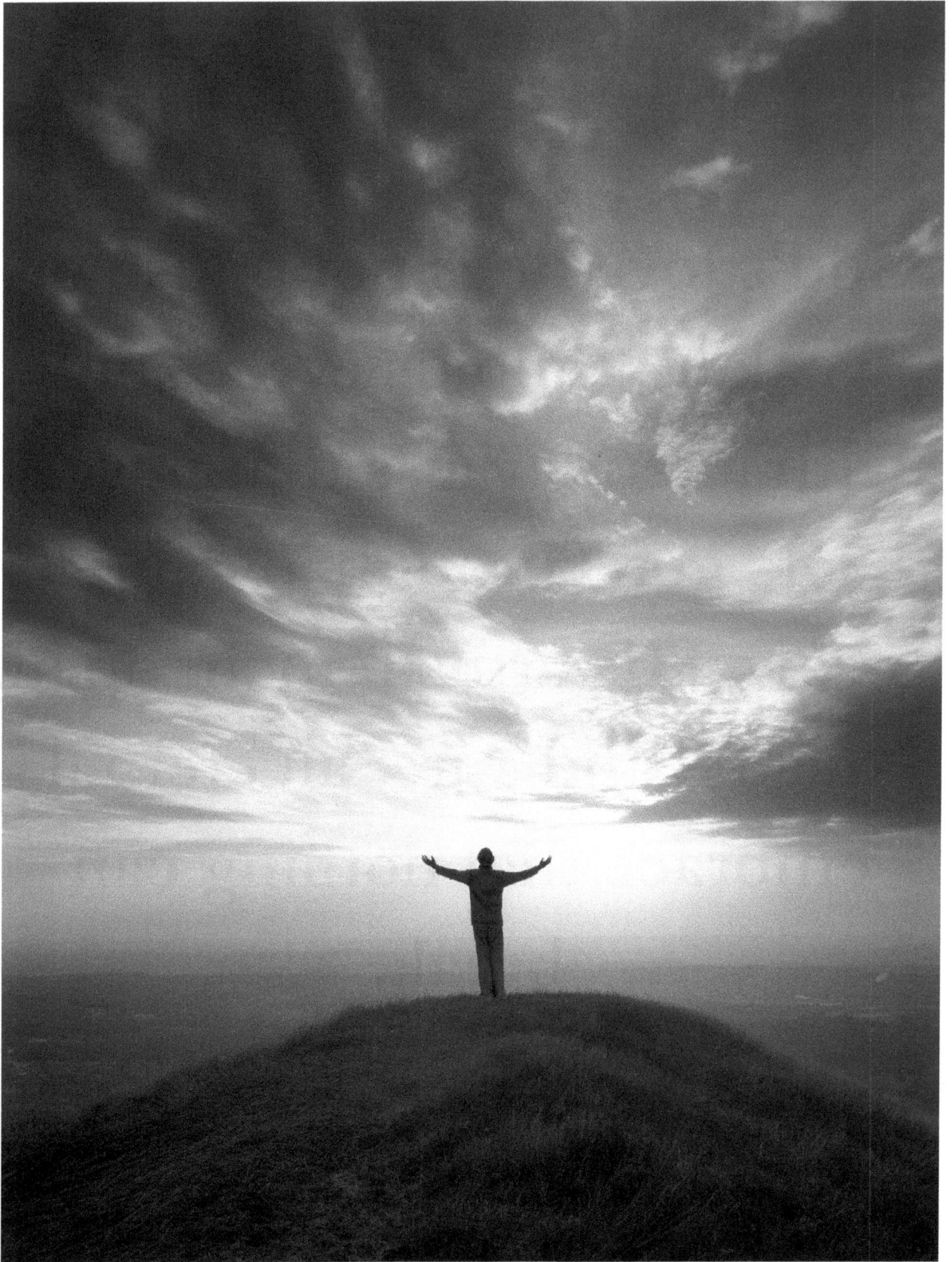

Grace is the miracle of God bending toward the broken. It gathers the scattered pieces of our lives and reshapes them into beauty we could not imagine. Where we see only failure, He sees the possibility of new creation. Every scar becomes a testimony of His healing, every weakness, a canvas for His strength. This grace does not simply forgive—it transforms, turning sorrow into song and despair into hope. It lifts the fallen, steadies the trembling, and writes a story of redemption over every chapter we thought was lost. In His hands, nothing is wasted; all is made new.

Grace falls freely, soaking even the driest heart with forgiveness and new life. Like a soft, steady rain it cleanses the past, refreshes the weary spirit, and nourishes hope until it blooms again.

From the dawn of creation to the cross and beyond, God's love has been a steady dance of giving and delight. He loves not because we are perfect but because He is, and His love never wearies or withdraws. To rest in that love is to find the freedom to forgive, to serve, to rejoice without fear. It calls us into a rhythm older than time, where every heartbeat meets His everlasting "yes," and every breath becomes an echo of His joy. This divine dance draws us near, teaching our hearts to move with grace and to live in the music of eternity.

———————————————————

Christ meets us not at our best but in our need, wrapping failure in His patient compassion. He bends low to lift the broken, turning our weakness into a testimony of His unfailing kindness and gentle strength.

Family is a living gift, a sacred circle where God's love first takes root and learns to speak. Within its embrace we are shaped, comforted, and stretched toward the fullness of who we are meant to be. Around the table and in the quiet of ordinary evenings, His presence weaves hearts together with cords of lasting mercy - threads of laughter, patient forgiveness, and unspoken prayer. Even when distances grow or seasons change, the bond formed by His grace endures, stronger than time or circumstance. In every shared memory and every act of care, we catch a glimpse of heaven's household, where the Father gathers His children and love is both beginning and endless home.

No distance, no darkness, no sin is beyond the reach of His boundless love. From the highest joy to the deepest ache, His affection follows, calling every heart back to the safety of His eternal care.

Life & Resurrection

n that first Easter morning the stone was rolled away and history changed forever. The grave could not hold the Son of God and death lost its final word. His victory is not distant but present, breathing life into every believer and filling each day with the power of renewal. Through Him every sorrow can be redeemed and every ending rewritten as a beginning filled with hope. Resurrection means that nothing, not grief, not failure, not darkness, has the last say when Christ is Lord, for His rising light reaches every shadow and His love continues to make all things new.

The empty tomb declares that death is not the end but the dawn of everlasting life. Christ's rising scatters every shadow, filling the world with the light of unending hope.

Resurrection is not only an event long past; it is the pulse of our present faith and the heartbeat of every redeemed moment. Each time we turn from despair to trust, from sin to grace, we share in Christ's rising and taste the victory of Easter anew. The Spirit who raised Jesus from the dead now breathes within us, awakening courage where fear once ruled, joy where sorrow lingered, and the freedom to begin again when all seemed lost. His life flows quietly through our ordinary days: strengthening weary hearts, renewing broken dreams, and assuring us that no night is final and no grave too deep for His love to reach. In every act of forgiveness, every step of faith, resurrection is happening still, a living promise that we are being made new until the everlasting morning dawns.

Because Christ lives, hope is never buried; it rises with Him and walks beside us each day. His victory turns every ending into a beginning and every sorrow into possibility.

The cross shows love willing to die; the resurrection shows love that cannot be destroyed. In Christ, life proves stronger than every fear, stronger than every sorrow, stronger than the weight of the grave itself. His rising shatters the power of darkness and speaks a final word of victory over every loss. The risen Savior walks beside us even now, steady in our uncertainty, gentle in our grief, turning our darkest nights into mornings bright with promise. Each new dawn carries the echo of that first Easter, reminding us that no wound is beyond His healing and no ending beyond His renewal. Because He lives, we can face tomorrow with courage, knowing that His life flows through us and that death has lost its claim forever.

Life in Christ is a season that never fades, a green promise that winter cannot hold. Even in the coldest moments, His Spirit stirs the soil of the soul toward bloom.

The story of resurrection is the story of God's unstoppable love. Love that steps into the deepest shadow and calls forth life where all seemed lost. Christ's victory is not confined to a single morning long ago; it reverberates through every heartbeat today, whispering that nothing is too broken for renewal. When we stumble under the weight of fear or grief, His risen presence draws near, lifting us with a power stronger than despair. In Him, endings become beginnings, ashes bloom into beauty, and every tear becomes a seed of joy. This is the eternal rising: the promise that light will always break the darkness, and that the life of Christ within us will never fade but carry us into a dawn that has no end.